Training Needs Analysis

in a week

TOM HOLDEN

Hodder & Stoughton

A MEMBER OF THE HODDER HEADLINE GROUP

Orders: please contact Bookpoint Ltd, 130 Milton Park, Abingdon, Oxon
OX14 4SB.
Telephone: (44) 01235 827720. Fax: (44) 01235 400454. Lines are open from
9.00–6.00, Monday to Saturday, with a 24 hour message answering service.
Email address: orders@bookpoint.co.uk

British Library Cataloguing in Publication Data
A catalogue record for this title is available from The British Library

ISBN 0 340 857730

First published 2002
Impression number   10 9 8 7 6 5 4 3 2 1
Year   2007 2006 2005 2004 2003 2002

Copyright © 2002 Tom Holden

Typeset by SX Composing DTP, Rayleigh, Essex.
Printed in Great Britain for Hodder & Stoughton Educational, a division of
Hodder Headline Plc, 338 Euston Road, London NW1 3BH by
Cox & Wyman Ltd, Reading, Berkshire.

CONTENTS

Acknowledgements

The Publishers and author would like to thank the following
for permission to reproduce extracts in this book:

Peter Honey Publications, Maidenhead, 2000.
www.peterhoney.com

■ I N T R O D U C T I O N ■

Training Needs Analysis (TNA) is a process that takes an identified organisational requirement and turns it into focused, effective and efficient training. To measure the success of the training an evaluation is also required. All training professionals will at sometime be required to conduct TNA. Many managers will be required to manage a project that requires training to be an integral part.

It does not look good if new equipment is introduced and no one can use it. It looks bad if a new process is not taught properly and leads to high levels of manufacturing waste. It is criminal if bad training, or the lack of training, leads to injury and death where health and safety is concerned.

The aim of this book is to provide a process which training professionals can use to produce a good TNA time and again. It is also designed to provide the client and project manager with an insight to what may be going on around them, their responsibilities to the analysts and their organisation, and ultimately to what they are paying for – for that is the bottom line today. Without a focused TNA, the training is wasted and so is any investment in it.

Why a Training Needs Analysis?

How many times has the need for training been recognised, welcomed by all and then criticised harshly after it has been delivered? Too many times? In any economic environment, it makes no sense to throw money at training. Training must be focused.

A Training Needs Analysis (TNA) is normally required when change takes place within the organisation. In most cases an outside 'driver' will create the need for change, although not all changes will lead to training; some changes may only lead to an amendment in a manual or a machine setting.

It is important for anyone involved with a TNA to be able to question the needs of the business, because the training need is derived from the business need. Therefore, today we will look at:

- A strategic definition of training
- A strategic definition of Training Needs Analysis (TNA)
- The 'change drivers' that could create a business need

Training defined

TNA has the specific objective of 'training':

- Derived from, and focused on, the business need
- Appropriate to the development of a specific individual or the organisation, in part or as a whole

Training has been defined many times over the years. The important elements are:

- Systematic development of the individual
- Attitude/knowledge/skill/behaviour pattern
- Perform adequately a given task
- Training must not develop the individual in a random fashion – it must be directed
- The training should improve specific characteristics of the individual
- The task will be directed and, subsequently, be assessed via the individual's performance 'on the job'

Due to the fact that organisational, as well as individual success, is now an important factor, the only way that success can be measured is through a properly planned and conducted evaulation process. We will look more closely at evaluation on Wednesday.

What is a TNA?

In its introduction to the TNA *Training and Development Checklist*, the Chartered Management Institute states that:

'Effective training or development depends more on knowing what results are required – for the individual, the department and the organisation as a whole. With limited budgets and the need for cost-effective solutions, all organisations need to feel secure that the resources invested in training are targeted at areas where training and development is needed and a positive return on the investment is guaranteed.

'Analysing what the training needs are is a vital

prerequisite for any effective training programme or event. Simply throwing training at individuals may miss the priority needs, and even cover areas that are not essential.'

Key elements within this definition are:

- Knowing what results are required – for the individual, the department and the organisation as a whole
- The need for cost-effective solutions
- Resources invested in training are targeted at areas where training and development is needed
- A positive return on the investment is guaranteed
- Analysing the training needs is a vital prerequisite
- Throwing training at individuals may miss the priority needs

Some key questions:

- What caused a need in the first place?
- How was the need recognised?
- What is the business need?
- What results are expected?
- When are the results expected?
- How will they be measured?
- Has the target population been correctly identified?
- Is there sufficient data for evaluation to take place?
- Will it be possible to demonstrate a return on investment (ROI)?
- What is the training need?

The TNA is a 'process stage' in the move from a business need to training and evaluation. We shall now look more deeply into the driving factors behind the business need in order to understand how the training need derives from, and focuses on, the business need.

Where the business need comes from

Training is change management. Furthermore, it is the management of change through changes in knowledge, skills, behaviour and attitudes.

When several aspects of the organisation's marketplace become subject to swift and large changes, a business's need for change becomes imperative. Many business needs will affect some or all of an organisation, and a training need will become obvious. We will refer to these marketplace changes as 'drivers'.

A TNA starts when a business case is put forward. Verbally or in writing, the business case is the response to the change drivers and it will argue for a training need. It is important to reiterate that not every business need will lead to a training need.

To ensure that we do not waste time, effort and money on ineffective or inappropriate training, the first step of the TNA should be to confirm the business need and to verify that a training need exists. This is done by gaining an understanding of the drivers that create the business need.

As we will see later this week, without an understanding of the business need, evaluation at the highest level cannot take place. You must understand what marketplace forces have affected the organisation to demonstrate return on investment (ROI). It is commonly accepted that the areas of change which have a major impact on organisations fall into four main categories:

- Economic
- Political
- Social
- Technological

We will spend the rest of today looking at the four categories and at some examples of appropriate training needs.

Economic changes

There are two types of economic change:

- Short term
- Long term

Short term

These operational changes may only affect a department or an individual by changing a small part of a process. They might lead to such a small change in working practices that no training is required. Operational, short-term and cyclical changes include:

Driver	Need
• Inflation	Business need – there will be an effect on sales Training need – unlikely, unless to make the sales department more competitive within the marketplace or to make the marketing department more effective
• Interest rates	Business need – accounts, and sales departments will need to adjust calculations Training need – unlikely
• Exchange rates	Business need – accounts and sales departments will need to adjust calculations Training need – unlikely

There are other changes that may have an effect. However, most managers deal with short-term change by fire-fighting.

Long term
Long-term drivers will have a strategic effect on business needs. They fall into four main categories:

- Growth rates
- Local and world marketplaces
- Local and community economies
- Competition – new and dying

GROWTH RATES

Despite ups and downs in the economy of a country or in the world, the underlying growth rate, or rate of fall, will affect spending capabilities. Changes in the underlying rate will have an effect on training needs: more money to spend; more goods and services being bought; more need for a trained workforce.

LOCAL AND WORLD MARKETPLACES

Technology changes have opened up the world marketplace. It makes sense that the larger the marketplace, the bigger the opportunity to sell and the greater the need for a trained workforce to meet its demands.

Increased competition will create a business need and then a multitude of training needs, possibly including new language skills.

COMMUNITIES AND NEIGHBOURING COUNTRIES

The European Union has opened the marketplace for countries that are local to and part of it. However, a marketplace with over 300 million people is a target to manufacturers from around the world. Being part of a 'community' may increase demand through protectionism, but it also creates a need to overcome multiple languages and cultural differences.

COMPETITION

The internet means that a new business is not just in competition with the local area, but also with the rest of the world. Nevertheless, it also means that, should an industry fail in one part of the world, it is possible to fill that hole and compete from a distance, or to expand existing business to plug the gap.

Political changes

The obvious political changes that take place within a country are the major elections. When one political persuasion replaces another, there are obvious effects upon areas, for example:

- *Legislation*: changes in health and safety.
- *Trade relations*: improved union laws lead to better working practices.
- *Public spending*: more or less on defence spending, social security or health.
- *Peace*: the ability to live peacefully internally and with neighbouring countries.

When countries make such changes, there may be a knock-on effect on bordering countries, trade agreements and political associations. Changes within one country will have effects upon its friends and enemies.

Increased defence spending in one country will lead to a response from those that feel threatened. It will also lead to a demand for more trained workers and scientists.

More positively, the removal of a threat will lead to increased market opportunities. If internal conflict is resolved, the country becomes open to development. If conflict between two or more countries is removed they become open to mutual development.

In all of the above cases, training is required because a political change driver has created a business need. Look at two major beneficial political changes that have taken place since 1985 and you will see that training needs were created.

• *Peace in Northern Ireland:*	Increased industry with more housing needed for the workforce. Trained builders and industry workforce required. Not so many glaziers required.
• *Unification of Germany:*	Changes in work practices, such as quality assurance, health and safety.

Bear in mind that political changes can also lead to attitude and behaviour change within an organisation. Some political changes will lead to indifference; others will lead to greater enthusiasm – a feeling of working for a higher cause.

Social changes

Social changes are one of the constants within modern-day society. They affect our attitudes, values and beliefs. All of which may affect our attitude and behaviour at work!

Examples of changes include:

Change	Business and training need
• Personal security	More burglar alarms need more trained staff to make, sell and install.
• Women's rights	Pay and work equality via new legislation will create a need for HR training
• Religion	Religious beliefs will require HR understanding with multi-cultural workforces
• The environment	Legislation will impose controls on chemical waste, for example, leading to management and handling training for workforce
• Health and safety	Major new legislation will lead to business needs and training needs, for example, maternity laws
• Population demographics	How do we spend our money? How age groups are defined? Who are the major purchasing groups? These are all questions that will affect business and training needs

Technological changes

Of all the changes we have looked at, technological changes provide the most obvious need for a TNA and evaluation. There are three main types of technological change:

- Changing what we make
- Changing the way we make and the way we distribute what we make
- Changing the way we communicate and store information

Changing what we make
There is a business need to stay competitive. A new product or service on the market creates a business need to better it. There is a need, therefore, for an ability to develop. Training in soft and hard skills is required to manufacture and sell new products, for instance, palm-top computers and DVDs. Existing products can be developed, such as multi-purpose mobile PDAs (Personal Digital Assistants) or phones, plasma TV/home cinema screens and mini-discs.

Changing the way we make and the way we distribute what we make
The way we manufacture our products is constantly changing. Workforces have to be trained to use the new processes. New quality tests and health and safety rules have to be passed on to the workforce through training.

In addition, what we make needs to get to market. Developments in this area might give an organisation the competitive edge on rival products and services, and allow the public access to services like online banking, shopping, etc.

Changing the way we communicate and store information
Our ability to communicate and store information is
constantly changing. Computers are getting smaller and
mobile phones are all around us. A business will be
uncompetitive if it is not using IT to some extent. Age is no
longer an excuse for an individual with a need to understand.

Essential technology
- E-mail
- Word processors
- Spreadsheets
- Databases
- The internet

Summary

Changes that affect an organisation fall into four main
categories:

- Economic
- Political
- Social
- Technological

The TNA cycle of events is:

- A change within the marketplace or organisation, which leads to a:
- Business need, which leads to a:
- Training need, which leads to a:
- TNA, which leads to:
- Evaluation, which could lead to:
- Going through the whole cycle again!

CHANGE   BUSINESS   TRAINING   TNA
DRIVER   NEED   NEED

The Training Needs Analysis process

Today we shall examine the TNA process at a strategic level, with an emphasis on the importance of sign off.

On Sunday we questioned the business need in order to confirm the origin of the training need. In doing so, we established the business need. A business need could include:

- A reduction of complaints
- The development of a new product
- A reduction in sickness rates
- The introduction of a new manufacturing process

Once you are satisfied that the training need is real, and is derived from the business need, you can begin to plan for the TNA process itself.

In order to plan, it is important to have the steps within the TNA process and its objectives in mind. Today we are going to look at learning styles and the operational steps that make up the TNA process, including the skills you will need to conduct or monitor the TNA.

The learning process

The TNA is an analytical process, which leads to learning. It seems obvious, but to understand the ultimate objective – the fact that people are going to learn – you need to understand how people learn.

A learning theory that provides an excellent understanding of how people learn, and which refined previous learning theories, is demonstrated in the Honey and Mumford Learning Styles Cycle and is shown below.

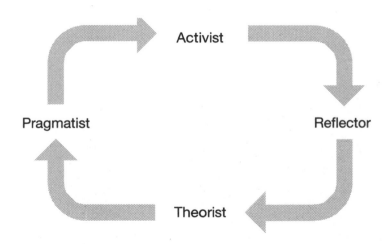

Based on the Honey and Mumford Learning Styles Questionnaire (1982,2000)

- *Activists*: become involved completely and objectively in new experiences. The immediacy of the experience is a contributory factor to the enjoyment.

- *Reflectors*: like to observe experiences from a distance and from different angles. Information and data, from personal experience and from others, is gathered and considered before reaching any conclusion.

- *Theorists*: their observations are modified and included within complicated, but rational, theories. Problems are approached in a hierarchical, logical way. They create their theories from a wide range of data.

- *Pragmatists*: like to try out their ideas, theories and techniques, testing them to see if they really work. They are always on the lookout for new ideas and are eager to be first to experiment.

In detail

It is vital to have a firm grasp of the TNA process. It will ensure that every time you conduct or monitor a TNA, you will be:

- Consistent, effective and efficient in conduct and output, delivering a focused service and without wasted effort or money
- Professional
- Confident
- Providing a quality service – because understanding the process will allow you to concentrate properly on the analysis process

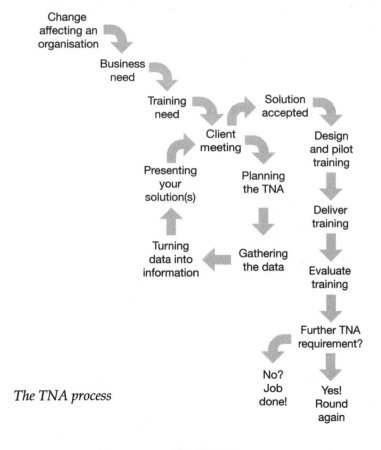

The TNA process

The steps to TNA Heaven

A good TNA needs to be based upon a model that can be repeated, maintaining consistency and effectiveness, but allowing the analyst freedom to produce a solution that focuses on the business need. A 'mobile' process can be applied to training needs as diverse as IT and time management.

Step 1: Questioning the business case and need
Ask to see the business case in order to understand the driver that created the business need. As will be shown on Wednesday, this phase and the data obtained from it will be important when evaluating Return on Investment (ROI).

Step 2: Deriving the training need
Having read the business case, you can now begin to see the objective – a strategic view of the business need. The training need is derived from this.

Step 3: Meeting the client
This first meeting, or set of meetings, between analyst and client or project manager is pivotal in ensuring that all parties are satisfied that the needs are communicated and understood.

Step 4: Planning the TNA
The outcome of this phase can be anything from a simple statement of how you intend to conduct the TNA to a detailed project plan. We will be looking more closely at this part of the process on Tuesday.

If evaluation is required, then the methods for collecting that data must be decided and agreed upon here. Evaluation will be discussed on Wednesday.

Step 5: Gathering the data

This phase, if planned properly, will provide the data from which the training solution is derived. Data gathering and any methodology will be covered on Thursday.

This is also an important phase for gathering pre-training evaluation data. Without this data it is impossible to look back and compare improvements, as we shall demonstrate on Wednesday.

Step 6: Turning data into information

The data gathered in the previous phase has to be sorted, interpreted and written into a report with solution(s). Software can be used to support this phase, as in the data collection phase. We will look at the transformation of data into information on Friday.

Step 7: Presenting your solution

The information gleaned from your data, the background to the whole TNA and your recommended solutions will be presented to the project manager or client in a format agreed. We will look at reports and their presentation on Friday.

Step 8: Completion of TNA

A final meeting where you hand over to the design team, unless you return to evaluate the training or, as a result of your observations, the project manager or client sees the potential for more work. The possible options available once the TNA is complete will be covered on Saturday.

Step 9: Evaluation?

We will be talking about planning, preparing and conducting training evaluation on Wednesday.

Hats to wear

As stated on Sunday, a TNA is mainly about change and knowledge management. However, there are other skills against which you should map yourself against to ensure that you have an understanding of the TNA. Other hats you will need to wear include the following.

Change manager's hat
We have looked at the causes of change previously. Now, we are going to look at how we handle change within the process of the TNA. This is important because the TNA itself is a change agent. The organisation has seen a need for change, which will require training. Therefore, the department or entire company will be forced to experience change. This means that change is being imposed on the workforce.

The two main characteristics of change are that it will always be here and that it is getting faster. A good manager should

be able to not just manage change, but significantly add to its implementation. However, with regard to the TNA itself, you will need to be your own project manager.

As you will see, there may be a plethora of emotions displayed while you gather your data or present your solutions. As the analyst, the TNA is your responsibility and you need to be aware of the implications of change. However, the manager is responsible for managing that change.

Chief knowledge officer's hat
It is agreed, within knowledge management circles, that there are two major types of knowledge held within an organisation. The two knowledge types we are interested in are:

- Explicit
- Tacit

EXPLICIT KNOWLEDGE
Explicit knowledge relating to your TNA is held within the large areas of documentation that all companies have, for

example, reports, training documentation and the initial business case itself.

TACIT KNOWLEDGE
This area of knowledge is much more subjective than explicit knowledge. It can be described as understood, but not well documented (if at all). It will not be couched in specific terms. People who work for or hold regular contact with the organisation hold this type of knowledge.

Although difficult to grasp, tacit knowledge is pivotal to knowledge management. If quantified and allowed to reach its full potential on a regular basis, it will prove an asset to any organisation.

Project manager's hat
Why is project management needed for a TNA? Well, because you will have to manage the analysis function, linking it in with all of the business needs, training needs and objectives. When it comes to the TNA, it is the analyst's responsibility to:

- Plan the analysis
- Organise the analysis
- Coordinate the analysis
- Control the analysis
- Lead the analysis

The plan should be presented to the client in an agreed format – written and discussed at a planning meeting.

The plan should then be 'signed-off' and, from that point, change control imposed. This means that any shift in the client requirements is logged and the risks and assumptions are stated, understood and agreed.

SIGN OFF, ASSUMPTIONS AND RISKS

These three elements of project management need emphasising because of the bearing they have on the TNA's progress.

- *Assumptions*: do not worry about stating the obvious here. It is important that you tell the project manager that you assume certain actions will occur on time.
- *Risks*: again do not worry about stating the obvious. If an action does not take place as expected then it will impact on the time taken to conduct the TNA.
- *Sign off*: vital to the progress of any TNA. If any stage of your work is not signed-off by the client or project manager, then you can not move on to the next stage.

  Indeed – you should not move to the next stage until the stage you have completed has been signed off.

Time manager's hat

Time management is a skill that we all need – all of the time! In the same way that you are going to have to project manage your TNA, you will need to meet the time deadlines agreed between you and the client in your project plan. We will re-emphasise the following points on Tuesday, but when you plan your projects you need to keep certain time elements in mind, for example:

- Long-term objectives
- Medium-term objectives
- Short-term objectives
- Milestones

All objectives should be SMART:

> S – Specific
> M – Measurable
> A – Achievable
> R – Realistic
> T – Time bounded

LONG-TERM OBJECTIVES

Long-term objectives can be as long or as short as the project itself, a month or a year. However, they should be represented in a simple statement and they should address the client's business need.

In business terms they might be expressed as a Mission Statement – a single sentence that sums up the long-term objective of the organisation. In analysis terms they should represent the training need, which should address the business need.

MEDIUM-TERM OBJECTIVES

These derive from the long-term objective. They should also be 'SMART'. Medium-term objectives break down the long-term objective into manageable and definable objectives. They define the 'critical path'. They should be associated with the relevant resource, such as the stakeholder, project manager, training manager, and client.

SHORT-TERM OBJECTIVES

These are the daily tasks in your analysis. These should also be 'SMART'.

MILESTONES

Recognised as a point which cannot be passed until certain objectives have been met, milestones are specific dates, or times, which are agreed between the analyst and client. They might represent:

- A decision or review date
- A sign-off date

SAVING TIME AT MEETINGS

Meetings should not take place without a clear reason for them. As the analyst, you will request meetings. Make sure that you have a set of objectives before requesting a meeting and do not be afraid to ask the purpose of a meeting called by the client or any stakeholders. The various objectives that might necessitate a meeting, and how you might prepare for them, will be discussed on Tuesday.

Other hats

You will need to be able to wear other hats to support the TNA process properly and we will be covering their input as we go through the week:

- Chief evaluator
- Researcher
- Training expert
- Customer relationship manager

Summary

Honey and Mumford recognised that there were four main learning styles:

- Activists
- Reflectors
- Theorists
- Pragmatists

The steps to TNA heaven are:

1 Questioning the business case and need
2 Deriving the training need
3 Meeting the client
4 Planning the TNA
5 Gathering the data
6 Turning data into information
7 Presenting your solution
8 Completion of TNA
9 Evaluation?

In order to conduct a TNA you will have to be a:

- Change manager
- Chief knowledge officer
- Project manager
- Time manager
- Chief evaluator
- Researcher
- Training expert
- Customer relationship manager

Planning the Training Needs Analysis

Now we have an overview, we can take our TNA observations a little deeper. We will be looking in more detail at the planning process, and at Force Field Analysis (as a tool to identify possible problems), milestones and deliverables.

Analyst and meetings

The first meeting with the project manager or client is to gather information. All analysts should:

- Prepare before a meeting. First check that there is a reason to hold the meeting.
- Make sure there is an agenda, even if it is just an e-mail stating the items to be discussed during the meeting. This statement will force all participants to focus on the need and validity of the meeting.
- Start the meeting if the client has requested you to.
- Control the meeting if the client has requested you to.
- Ensure that the client has a true record of the proceedings of the meeting – decisions, actions and dates for those actions to be completed.
- End the meeting professionally. Ensure that if another meeting is required, all parties agree a date, time and place. Even if there is dispute, a meeting to resolve issues should be arranged.
- After the meeting the analyst should record actions and deadlines and make sure that they are agreed and circulated amongst all relevant meeting attendees.

A typical example of information you may already have is:

- The request for the TNA – telephone conversation, e-mail or letter and associated notes
- Desk research – internet research
- Initial business case

First meeting
The main purposes of the first meeting are to check information you already have, to clarify the need and to gain information that relates to the TNA objective, and that helps you to conduct the TNA itself.

Though some of your questions may have been answered by information you have already been given, you might ask:

- For clarification of the business need
- For the training need
- For dates
- Who are the major stakeholders?

- Who is the sign-off authority?
- In order to support the training need:
  - How many people need to be trained?
  - Where do they work – number of sites?
  - What are their roles and positions?
  - Is there a different training need for different roles and positions?
  - Is it an IT roll-out, a soft skill or both?
- In order to support the TNA administration:
  - Where is the training to take place?
  - Is e-Learning an option?
  - Does the organisation have the infrastructure – the intranet – to support e-Learning?
  - How often to report, who to and in what format?
- Will evaluation be required?

There will be many more, project-specific questions for you to think of.

Once the meeting has concluded and you have returned to the office confident that you have all the information you need, get some written agreement from the project manager or client that they feel confident that you understand their 'need'.

The TNA plan

A project can be defined as:

- Unique
- The responsibility of a team or of a person with all of the team's skills

- A change agent
- Having a specific objective
- Time bounded
- Consuming resources, time and costs

A TNA shares all of these characteristics and is, therefore, a project. This means that we should approach its planning in a similar fashion.

The minimum information supplied within the TNA plan should be:

- A start date for the complete TNA
- An end date for the complete TNA – this should allow time for development of training documentation, pilot training, setting up of classrooms, training of trainers, etc.
- A statement of the number of days between start date and end date – the days may not be consecutive
- A start date for each of the phases
- An end date for each of the phases
- A statement of the number of days between those dates – the work may not use consecutive days
- Milestone dates for meetings, delivery of reports, questionnaires and their sign off
- Role, number and level of client's staff to be sent a questionnaire and/or interviewed
- The type of interview, for example, one-to-one or group – the advantages and disadvantages will be highlighted below
- Any resources required – who needs to attend meetings, provide support – stakeholders, subject

matter experts, third parties
- Any meetings to finalise training plan – some project managers need help in planning training events, the development of the training documentation might be done by a third party, etc.
- Post-training evaluation – if agreed, set a date or dates for post-training evaluation
- Risks and assumptions should be stressed throughout – do not be afraid of stating the obvious

The TNA plan, when completed, should be presented to the client in an agreed format – as discussed at the first meeting.

The plan should then be 'signed off' and, from that point, change control imposed.

Change control
Change control means that any changes to the agreed plan will be logged, the risks and assumptions stated, understood and agreed. Moreover, any impact on time-scales and costs will have to be renegotiated. Make sure that you are realistic in your planning. Nothing destroys your credibility with the client more than to keep asking for more time. Unless, of course, the client instigates the change, then change control works in your favour.

Planning the data gathering
Data gathering starts from the moment you are approached with the task – never go into a meeting or interview unprepared. However, once the TNA begins, the official data-gathering phase must be planned.

A good tool for planning the data gathering and preparing

yourself for the reactions to the TNA is Force Field Analysis (FFA).

Force Field Analysis
A successful TNA, using FFA, is based upon knowledge of the objective and the change to be implemented.

The business case will provide the reason for the change; the FFA will help you to find the best way to achieve the change.

FFA works on the assumption that any change takes place within the working environment against a background of people with their priorities, relationships, attitudes and values. You also need to understand the arena in which the change is to occur.

Force Field Analysis divides the 'forces' you will encounter and that you need to harness, in order to complete the process. They are:

Forces which move you towards a successful TNA completion, for example:

- Commitment from the top
- Communication
- Working with those directly affected
- The resources to do the job

Forces or obstructions which stop you achieving a successful TNA, for example:

- Resistance from stakeholders
- Resistance from the workforce
- Lack of communication
- Lack of resources

This phase creates the yardsticks to measure against in post-training evaluation. If the appropriate skills and behaviours are not correctly identified and tested, then the effects of the training may be meaningless or even worthless. Ask yourself:

- Why am I collecting the data?
- Knowing the training need, what do you need to know?
- What methods shall I use?
- How can I ensure that the data is valid and reliable?

This phase will require planning inputs for:

- *Questionnaire development and sign off*: it is not uncommon for the client to add questions that might be unrelated to the training purpose of the questionnaire. You must make sure that questions are appropriate and focused, ensuring that you will get the correct response to the questions asked.
- *Distributing questionnaires*: who is going to distribute them? Will a master copy be sent to a single point within the client organisation then copied and distributed? Will the questionnaire be sent to each person by e-mail?
- *Site visits*: get the client to arrange meetings with stakeholders, provide interviewees, etc. You need to state how many sites you wish to visit, whether you need to stay overnight and what expenses there will be.
- *Conducting interviews*: this is can be done with members of the client organisation who have completed questionnaires.
- *Observation*: excellent for assessing 'attitude' and 'behaviour'. Plan and test any recording methodology.
- *End product*: will you need to see what is 'produced' – the

'end product'? Is the training intended to affect the quality of this product?

- *Desk research*: the use of data that has already been collected for other purposes. This use of explicit knowledge is sometimes referred to as secondary research. The phrase comes from academic terminology referring to:
  Primary sources: actual data from research, first-hand accounts of events, which are used in your research.
  Secondary sources: conclusions drawn from third parties. For example, the use of autobiographies to draw second-level conclusions.
- *Pre-training evaluation*: this will be discussed further when looking at the industry standard for evaluation – the Kirkpatrick model. Nevertheless, there may be a need for testing behaviour skills at this point. The test methodology should be agreed with the client and, if need be, signed off.

Planning how to turn data into information
This is a vital phase and forms the basis of the data gathering outcomes. It is often the case that you have had a reasonable idea for the solution from day one. However, avoid preconceptions – wait until you have the data in front of you. You might be keen on e-Learning for instance, but this will be no good if the infrastructure does not exist within the client organisation.

How the data is collated depends upon the data that is collected. The responses to the questionnaires and interviews will affect the decision to use one or all of the following:

- A pie chart
- A list of comments
- A table of percentages

Certainly, reports do benefit from some form of graphic display of data.

Planning the report writing
There are many kinds of report that provide analysis. A TNA provides a report, or reports, which should contain:

- Training solutions
- Training design specifications

TNA report in general
We will be returning to this document later in the week but, as a set of general headings, you might include details of the:

- Client organisation (a description)
- Initial request for TNA
- Initial business case (or key extracts from it)
- Project plan – though this could be an Appendix if wished
- Data-gathering techniques
- Data collation tools
- Data gathering within client organisation
- Results of data gathering

- Solutions (provide options – up to three), with risks and assumptions stated
- Recommended solution (from three) – with risks and assumptions stated
- Appendices with example questionnaire or any detailed data that expands on the data results shown earlier

Training solutions
A strategic view of the training solution(s) may be all that the client requires and we shall look at possible options for training on Friday. The solutions, unless agreed otherwise, should be strategic.

These solutions should be followed by a brief description of content.

Design Specifications
This may be a stand-alone document in its own right, but is often included within the TNA report. It takes the recommended strategic solution description and provides a more detailed explanation of, amongst other things,

- Content – detailed, complete description of the training
- Learning environment – classroom, intranet or internet online modules
- Training timings – one-day workshop
- Design timing – how many days to complete a development task
- Costings – designer rates, any other resource costs
- Input from third parties – Subject-Matter Experts (SMEs)
- Input from client organisation – project manager, the

client may be the SME
- Such information that is transferable from the TNA report

Planning how to present the report
The form of the report presentation is decided between the analyst and client. This can include the following:

- E-mailed document with covering e-mail
- Posted document with covering letter
- PowerPoint presentation of solutions in front of one or more members of the client organisation
- A combination of the above or more

What is important is that the method of delivery is agreed at the start of the TNA.

Planning the evaluation
A properly conducted TNA, focused on the business and training needs of the client, will go a long way to being cost-effective and efficient. However, if proper evaluation is conducted, it can be proven whether the results are successful or not.

If the client agrees to full evaluation, it should be conducted at times agreed between the client and analyst. The number of times that evaluation is conducted, and how long after training it takes place, should be agreed and planned for. If post-training evaluation is conducted it is to consider:

- What has been learned – skills and knowledge
- If behaviour and attitude have changed
- If there is a return on investment (ROI)

You may have noticed that any reaction to training has not been included in the above list. If you are the trainer you will certainly want to include this. If the client requests that you, the analyst, conduct this phase of evaluation then you will need to plan for this as well.

We will look at all of these stages in the evaluation process, and when to prepare for them, when we look at the Kirkpatrick model for the evaluation of training tomorrow.

Stating the risks and assumptions

It is vital, at every opportunity, to make a list for the client of any risks and assumptions that are related to actions and solutions within the analysis process.

The major consequence of any of the risks occurring is that time will be wasted and the analysis process delayed. It might seem obvious to state risks and assumptions, but they protect both client and analyst throughout the process.

Summary

The TNA process needs to be planned to ensure that all parties involved are sure that the training is focused on the needs of the organisation. The first meeting sets the tone and success of the TNA. As the analyst you will need to control the meeting and gather such information that will allow you to plan the process of analysis. Make sure you get the dates, numbers, stakeholders and sign-off authorities. Keep in mind the old rhyme of 'which, what, where, when, who, etc' and you will not go wrong.

Evaluation techniques

Good planning is vital to the success of any project and TNA is no different. Moreover, proper evaluation of training is vital to confirm the TNA's success. It is only human for all participants in the process to want to know how well the training went and what changes and benefits have been achieved.

Evaluation should also be used to ensure the quality and effectiveness of training and, ultimately, to give credence to the role of training itself.

Yesterday we looked at the planning process in more detail and it included the planning of, and preparation for, evaluation. Today we shall look at evaluation in much more detail, and in particular at the points within the TNA process:

- **Planning** for evaluation
- **Preparing** for, and **conducting** the evaluation

There are many reasons for evaluating training, but here we shall concentrate on the purpose of feedback.

Training evaluation experts such as Donald Kirkpatrick (1967) and Warr, Bird and Rackham (1970) provided an evaluation on four levels, each becoming more complex. Later, Hamblin (1974) redefined the uppermost level and effectively created a fifth.

Evaluation point	Kirkpatrick	Warr, Bird and Rackham	A C Hamblin
Training	Level 1 – reaction to training Level 2 – what was learned?	Reaction to training Immediate evaluation	Reaction to training What was learned?
On-the-job	Level 3 – changes in behaviour	Intermediate evaluation	Changes in job behaviour
Performance changes within the organisation	level 4 – results	Ultimate evaluation	Organisation changes
Culture			Level 5 – ultimate

The purpose of this chapter is to provide a practical insight into the opportunities for planning, the data you might need to request or obtain, and the post-training evaluation opportunities you will need to prepare for.

Planning for evaluation

The initial impression of 'post-training evaluation' is that the work will be done after the training has taken place. However, to complete training evaluation at its highest and most complex level requires you to return to the start of the whole process – the change that initially created the business case. Evaluation is a 'pre' and 'post'-training experience.

To successfully plan for evaluation, you need to know where the planning points are in the TNA process. First, be aware that evaluation should be as objective a process as you can possibly make it, because it will be open to subjectivity on the part of everyone involved. Training evaluation has to be applied to an individual's:

- Response to training (subjective)
- Practical ability to do their job (objective)
- Knowledge of how they do their job (subjective and objective)
- Way they think about how they do their job (subjective and objective)
- Manner in which they do their job (subjective and objective)

Effective and realistic evaluation it can be based upon one of two approaches:

1 Evaluation without historical comparison

This method requires either:
- An agreed standard set between yourself and the client
- The standard set by an outside agency, such as a professional body, or set by a legal requirement, such as the law on health and safety

2 Evaluation by historical comparison

This method requires you to gather information for comparison either from the client, or using your own methods during the TNA process. We will cover some methods of data gathering later.

Evaluation planning point 1
The first evaluation planning point in the TNA process happens before you start. The client will have made some internal observations, for instance:

- Drop in sales
- Increase in complaints
- Increase in product return
- Change in marketplace (see Sunday)

These observations will have led to a business case, resulting in the business and training needs.

If the client asks for or agrees to evaluation, this will be your first planning point and it directly affects any successful evaluation at the highest level – the 'Results' or 'Ultimate' level as it is referred to. This is the level at which ROI is calculated or organisational cultural change is measured.

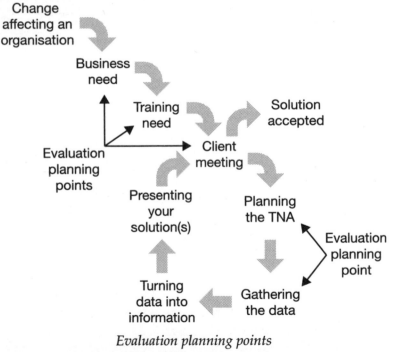

Evaluation planning points

Evaluation planning point 2
Having agreed to evaluate the training, the next planning point takes place before any data is gathered. Your project plan will indicate when you will evaluate and how much time you will spend on preparing and gathering the data, but it will not show how you intend to measure and gather. You would gather data by observation, question and testing for comparison in skills, knowledge, attitude and behaviour Immediate and Intermediate levels (Kirkpatrick, Warr, Bird and Rackham).

Other evaluation planning points
A good analyst should always be aware of the need:

- For good evaluation planning
- To recognise every opportunity to gather data for later evaluation purposes

You will also need to plan for the post-training evaluation process itself, for example:

• Timing of evaluation	At an agreed time-scale between you and the client or project manager – it may be a single or multiple visit immediately after the training or some time later when results can be seen over a length of time
• Location of evaluation	Normally within the workplace, but you might find that a simulation away from the workplace is better, safer, not so distracting, etc.

- Level of   This will be influenced by the amount
  evaluation   of pre-training data gathered and the
                  level agreed between you and the
                  client or project manager

Preparing for and conducting the evaluation

There are a number of points you need to prepare for the
evaluation process:

- Agreeing the level of evaluation
- Gathering historical data if required
- Researching the explicit knowledge held within the
  client organisation
- Researching the tacit knowledge held within the
  client organisation
- Compiling questionnaires
- Preparing observation sheets
- Gathering examples of the 'end product'

The above is not an exhaustive list, but should give you some
indication of the size of the task if it is to be done properly.

Preparation point 1
This is done as soon as you are contacted and asked to do the
TNA or resourced to the task.

This level of evaluation, where ROI needs to be defined, is
often avoided because of the following:

- There are no defined 'yardsticks' or data against
  which to measure

- External factors, other than training, can distort the result
- To evaluate a department's performance usually means evaluating a group of people – the mix of skills within the department can distort measurements.

It is very difficult to demonstrate an improvement in sales or a reduction in complaints if there are no sales figures or records of complaints on which to base the performance measurement. The data must be clearly identified, unambiguous and accessible. A good analyst will:

- Identify the appropriate data, such as:
  - Sales figures
  - Disciplinary records
  - Complaints records
  - Health and safety records
  - Customer numbers.

- Where the data is not available (in a business case or in research conducted by the client) gather it, in a manner that is appropriate to the data and its source. Impossible if the time-scales for action are short, but quality data is worth proper planning and preparation, and will show training benefits and results.

- Agree with the client or project manager the time-scales for evaluation.

Immediately after the training will not allow sufficient credible data to be gathered. Depending upon the type and source of the data it may be 6 months before the evaluation can take place avoiding, for example, seasonal variations.

Preparation point 2

This falls immediately prior to, and within, the data-gathering phase. This evaluation preparation is vital for an objective demonstration of improvement in:

- Skills
- Working knowledge
- Attitude to the job
- Behaviour in conducting the job

There are degrees of complexity and preparation for these four elements, which we have split into three headings:

1 Practical – the skills needed to do the job
2 Cognitive – the knowledge required to do the job
3 Emotional – the attitude that reinforces the behaviour of the person doing the job

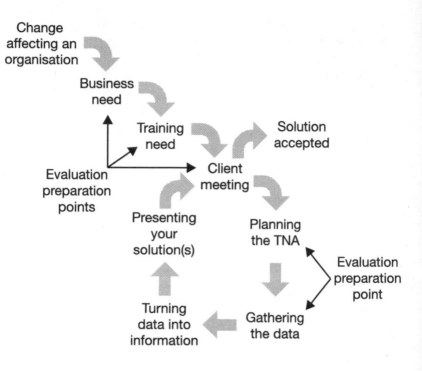

Evaluation preparation points

Preparing for and evaluating the training day
This evaluation will take place on the day of training. It is normally the responsibility of the training deliverer to gather and process this data at the request of the client. Often the analyst does not get involved. It is traditionally referred to as 'Reaction' level evaluation and takes the form of a questionnaire.

The 'Happy Sheet', as it is unprofessionally often referred to, will contain questions relating to:

- The trainer's training skill
- The trainer's knowledge
- The quality of training documentation
- Course objectives being met
- Personal objectives being met
- The training environment
- The course administration

These questions are generally asked using scales and often produce unrealistic data.

Problems that can be encountered are when delegates:

- Feel they have not had time to assess training documentation
- Do not have the knowledge to assess the trainer
- Are nervous about completing the form
- Are often subjective in their evaluation
- Mark down the training environment when it is on company property

Preparing for and conducting practical (skills) evaluation
The vast amount of actions evaluated under this heading will be manual. The term 'practical skill' refers to an individual's ability to create, repair, manufacture, etc. There are two main methods of skills evaluation which are conducted back in the workplace post-training:

1 Observation

Which requires:
- Planning of forms and scoring system
- The observer having the skill which is being evaluated
- The ability to observe in the workplace or within a simulated, realistic environment

2 End Product

Which requires:
- A plan against which the end product can be measured
- A scoring system
- An example of the end product
- The person evaluating having the skill to assess the end product

Some advantages and disadvantages of each method are:

1 Observation

Advantages:
- Seeing the skill being used within the workplace
- Seeing the skill being used 'warts and all'

Disadvantages:
- Requires cooperation of the person using the skill
- The person being observed might find the process daunting

2 End Product

Advantages:
- Not watching the skill being used may allow the person to be more relaxed
- A more realistic product might be produced

Disadvantages:
- Mistakes may be covered up
- The end product may be the best of a number produced
- The person creating the 'end product' may make an effort to produce a better quality of work

Skills evaluation should:

- Ensure that an agreed or required level of competence has been achieved
- Measure an improvement in learning

A good analyst, when evaluating skills, would ensure that:

- The level of evaluation is agreed between the client and project manager
- The skill and its make-up is identified
- Where possible, observation and end product evidence is decided upon during the data gathering for post-training evaluation
- The observation process is firm and consistent (there may be more than one person to observe)
- A standard template is used for the observation form that supports the process
- The process and the template have been piloted by themselves, an independent expert and the client organisation
- Skilled observers were used – all of the time
- All concerned are happy with the location

Preparing for and conducting cognitive (knowledge) evaluation
If a product is produced consistently to a high standard, there must not only be a skill but also the knowledge of how the end product is made. However, to test the 'knowledge' component requires a different set of evaluation techniques. Observation may not reveal knowledge of a process, but merely repetition.

Knowledge is evaluated by questioning in the workplace, some time after training is completed. Some forms that the evaluation might take are:

Written
- Questionnaires (yes/no answers)
- Multiple-choice question paper
- Short answer question paper
- Conventional exam

Oral
- Interview
- Interview using set questions
- Oral examination

Questionnaires and interviews will be discussed later in the week. Examples of knowledge we might evaluate are:

- Simple processes
- Simple procedures
- Health and safety
- Work regulations
- Complex processes
- Complex reactions

It is important to note that the more limited the response required, the easier it is to mark the response – but the more difficult it is to 'set' the questions. The more open and free the response, the easier it is to set the question – but the more difficult it is to mark.

There are advantages and disadvantages to both written and oral forms of knowledge evaluation, but a good analyst will make sure that:

- The level of evaluation is agreed between the client and project manager

- All components of the knowledge to be tested are identified
- Where relevant, knowledge is tested before training for comparison after training
- Any question paper is piloted – multiple-choice questions completed by someone with the knowledge and someone without will provide a 'control' response
- A standard set of questions are used when supporting the interview process
- The process and questions have been piloted by themselves, independent expert(s) and the client organisation
- Skilled interviewers and markers were used – all of the time
- Markers and interviewers are briefed to ensure standard marking and questioning

Preparing for and conducting emotional (attitude and behaviour) evaluation

For the purpose of this book, the attitude and behaviour evaluation requirements are discussed together. Common practice includes 'attitude' with skill and knowledge at the level often referred to as 'immediate', and 'behaviour' at a level of its own, referred to as 'intermediate'. It is accepted that attitude can affect behaviour and behaviour can affect attitude. But, when being knowingly observed, we tend to act 'appropriately'. So for the purpose of this book:

- Behaviour is seen as the outward display of emotions evaluated pre and post-training

- Attitude is the emotion motivating the behaviour display

ATTITUDE

It is recognised that training has very little effect on attitude. It is a characteristic that is extremely subjective and very difficult to evaluate. It is often hidden because people know how to respond within certain situations. We may hide our dislike of dealing with customers because we 'know' how to act when initially confronted by one. However, should we be pressurised in some way, we may reveal our attitude.

BEHAVIOUR

How a task is conducted, a customer dealt with and a telephone answered can be evaluated both pre and post-training by observation using trained and skilled observers.

It is commonly agreed that the trainee, trainer and organisation must work together for behavioural changes to occur. The person being trained must want to change. The trainer must ensure that the trainee knows what changes are required and how the changes can be achieved. The organisation they work for must provide a climate where change can take place and is rewarded.

To provide an opportunity for the trainee to change when back in the workplace:

- Management must allow the new skills or knowledge to be put into practice
- Equipment must be provided
- Roles must be changed
- Rewards must be given when the changes are made and maintained

Behavioural evaluation can be conducted by:

- The trainee – using a questionnaire
- Their line manager – using an observation interview
- An independent assessor – using an observation interview

The use of questionnaires is discussed fully later in the week. However, they might include questions on the following:

- The number of times a skill or knowledge was used
- View of self-competence pre-training
- Management's view of the trainee's competence pre-training
- Views held by both post-training
- Is the correct equipment in place for the change to occur?
- Has management supported the change?

Preparing for and conducting business return evaluation

Many organisations avoid this level of evaluation, often referred to as the 'Results' or 'Ultimate' level. The calculations involved should prove that the training has been beneficial to the organisation and that it has demonstrated a ROI (Return on Investment). Many other organisations have specific departments set up do just this task.

It was stated at the beginning of this chapter that evaluation was planned and prepared for right at the start of the TNA. ROI is evaluated right at the end of the process because it is seen as the final justification for the training. Some examples of costs to be considered when planning and calculating training are:

- Salaries of delegates attending
- Loss of revenue opportunities
- Travel expenses
- Cost of training
- If held on own site – cost of training room
- Training equipment – IT hire
- Training analysis
- Training course development – if bespoke
- Training documentation – again if bespoke

The list is not exhaustive!

Examples of benefits to be considered when planning and calculating training are:

- Increase in sales revenue over the agreed period
- Decrease in absenteeism

- Decrease in disciplinary interviews
- Increase in quality
- Decrease in complaints

The list is not exhaustive!

Some of the above are difficult to quantify, hence the reluctance of many analysts and organisations to attempt this exercise. However, proving and achieving ROI is becoming a major factor in the placement of consultancy contracts. By recognising the business need at the start and by using the data that instigated that need, the analyst should be able to prove ROI. It has been recognised that this level of evaluation can be split into two:

- Return on Investment (ROI)
- Changes within the culture of the organisation

Where it is difficult to prove ROI, it might be easier to demonstrate that the 'culture' of the organisation has changed for the better. Demonstrating a decrease in disciplinary interviews may be simpler than calculating their financial effect. This could be called 'Return on Emotional Investment' (ROEI).

However, for those who wish to calculate ROI, a formula that can be used is:

$$ROI = \frac{(Benefits - Costs)}{Costs} \times 100$$

Results
- A positive answer – the training has been a success
- A negative answer – the training has been unsuccessful
- Zero – break-even

Summary

For success in the evaluation phase you should:

- **Plan** for evaluation
- **Prepare** for, and **conduct** the evaluation

Collecting the facts

Samples, questionnaires and interviews

Today we shall examine the different types of questionnaire and interview you will use within the TNA. We will evaluate the advantages and disadvantages of both. We will also look at how you decide whether an individual or group will best supply your data.

The use of questionnaires within a TNA is commonplace. Here you will be assessing more:

- Who to ask – sample size, role and position
- How to ask – questionnaires and interviews

For any TNA there will be two levels of information gathering:

- Strategic – information that will help you run the TNA
- Training Needs Analysis-specific – information that moves you towards the training

Strategic information – business need

Strategic information forms the business need and is behind the training need. It will mostly come to you via an interview with the project manager or the client, and from the business case. Strategic information consists of example facts about the change, reasons behind the change and conduct concerning what is to be changed, for example:

Facts
- What type of hardware or software is to be introduced?
- What type of 'soft skill' training is required?
- Who will be affected? How many people will need training?
- Where will the changes take place? How many sites are affected?
- When is the intended change to take place?
- How soon prior to any hardware/software roll-out is the training needed?
- How many days are available for development?

Reason
- Why are the changes taking place?

Conduct
- Best practice
- Processes

These lists are not exhaustive.

You will need this information to create the project plan at the start of the TNA process, from the point the client recognises the need for change through to the creation of your plan for the TNA.

Training Needs Analysis-specific

Having created the project plan, the next phase is to concentrate on the training solution or, more properly, to concentrate on gathering the data that will lead you towards a client-focused training solution.

When using a questionnaire for IT training analysis, for example, the probability is that you will want to know facts about the training need, the beliefs and reasons behind the training need, and the conduct concerning the training need.

Facts
- What type of hardware or software is to be introduced?
- Who will be affected – what roles?
- Where will the changes take place?
- When is the intended change to take place?

Belief
- What is the individuals' perception of their own skill base?
- What level of importance do they place on a certain skill?

Reason
- Why are the changes taking place?

Conduct
- Best practice
- Processes

These lists are not exhaustive.

Deciding who to ask

As discussed, the knowledge and data you will require to conduct the TNA will fall into the following categories:

Strategic
- Explicit – held within organisation documentation, etc.
- Tacit – held by those directly controlling or affected by the TNA

TNA-specific
- Explicit – held within previous training documentation, detailed processes, etc.
- Tacit – held within the skills and knowledge of the workforce

Gathering data for the strategic elements of the TNA will involve a small number of people. You might want to speak to:

- The client or project manager
- Stakeholders
- Representatives of those affected
- Customers of the client's organisation

Primary research

There is a distinct process for 'primary research, as opposed to 'Secondary' or 'Desk' research. Primary deals with the discovery of the facts yourself. Secondary means that you are relying upon sources where someone else has discovered the facts, and you are interpreting or using their findings. The four steps are:

1 Sampling
2 Questionnaires
3 Types of question
4 Piloting

Sampling

Sampling allows the analyst to extract relevant data without having to approach the entire workforce. It then allows the analyst to extrapolate that data to the workforce as a whole. If carried out on an appropriate sample 'frame', accurate results can be achieved. The two most commonly used methods of sampling are:

- Random or probability sampling
- Quota or non-probability sampling

It is not uncommon to use a combination of both sample groups within a TNA. An effective sample frame would be:

- Accurate – no copies of sample targets or questions
- Complete – it would not leave out relevant targets or data
- Up to date
- Relevant to the objectives of the TNA
- Accessible

Random or probability sampling

With this type of survey, each member of the target sample has an equal chance of being selected. People within the workforce would be randomly sampled for questionnaire or interview, or both.

Obviously, there is a trade-off arising from the decision of how many people to include in the sample frame. One hundred per cent accuracy can only be obtained by targeting everyone in the workforce, therefore:

- Sample size should be agreed and stated within the project plan
- Risks should be made clear to the client or project manager – the smaller the sample, the less accurate the analysis
- Risks and assumptions, such as cost and time implications should be stated and agreed within the project plan

This method, with its comparison of sample frame to full population, establishes valid statistics and accurate data.

Quota or non-probability sampling
This method has a sample frame based upon subjective decisions of what is representative. This should be assessed by the analyst, and then agreed between analyst and client. For example, the analyst and client may choose a sample based on who is affected by the proposed changes – in terms of role, position, rank, and task. The advantages of this approach are:

- Costs – lower because the sample is precisely targeted
- Speed – quicker, for the same reason

Questionnaires

It is unlikely that you will place a questionnaire in front of a client or project manager in the initial interview, but you might want a list of questions to ensure that the main points are covered. Keep in mind the objectives of the data gathering whether the questions you intend to ask are from a list in front of you when at interview, or in a questionnaire form.

Questionnaire tips

Questions
Keep them straightforward and use plain language where possible – avoid ambiguity.

Level of question
Ensure you use an appropriate level of question. Do not insult the target, nor make the question too difficult.

Order of questions
Keep the order of the questions logical.

Practical points
- Use an introduction – do not forget to put in a reason for the survey and state the value of the response
- Use clear type and reasonable quality paper
- Leave room for comments and codes
- Ensure only questions relevant to the objectives of the TNA are asked
- If there are separate instructions for target and

> analyst, make sure that they are marked
> - Remember to thank the person for completing the questionnaire

Types of question

The two basic types of question asked at interview and in questionnaires are open and closed.

Open questions
These tend to lead to more detailed and subjective responses. They can be of many different types:

> - Unstructured – the response is completely free
> - Sentence completion – I consider this training to be . . .

An advantage of these answers is that they are less likely to be biased. A disadvantage is that they can be long-winded.

Closed questions
This is probably the type of question you will use when testing knowledge and skills of the workforce. They can be:

> - Multiple-choice questions – difficult to do and will need extensive piloting to ensure accuracy and appropriateness
> - Yes/No questions
> - Scales

Scales
There are two main types of scale questions, most obvious in their use within Gap Analysis (see below). They are:

- **The Likert Scale**
- **Importance Scale**

THE LIKERT SCALE

The sample is given a statement and then asked to state how much they agree or disagree.

No Skills	Not Bad	Average	Quite Good	Brilliant

IMPORTANCE SCALE

This scale is used, as is the Likert Scale, in Gap Analysis, to test the importance placed on a task or skill as perceived by the sample, or to test how often they use a skill.

Never	Seldom	Sometimes	Often	Always

Gap Analysis

This technique combines two or more scales to provide a 'skill gap'. If a value of 'average' (numerically 3 out of 5) is placed upon a skill, such as the ability to carry out a mail merge in Microsoft Word, using Microsoft Excel as a database, but respondents see themselves as 'often' (numerically 4 out of 5) carrying out the task, then there is a gap of 1 between perceived skill and the need to carry out the task.

Piloting

Never release a questionnaire unless it has been tested thoroughly. The same can be said for a question. There is no harm, if you are unsure, in piloting your list of questions in exactly the same way you would a questionnaire. Not only does it maintain the professional image, it ensures that the questions are focused. Some points to look for when piloting the questionnaire include:

- Respondents' understanding – are the questions and language clear?
- Difficulty in answering – is the answer system clear?
- Problems in the question order – logical?
- Respondent interest and attention span – too long, lose interest

- Effectiveness of filter questions and skip answers – 'If you do not need this skill, then move on to question 5'
- Ease of response analysis – make it easy for yourself

Interviews

When gathering the data, you will not rely purely on questionnaires and is unlikely that you will rely purely on interviews. You will probably mix the two methods.

There are three types of interview you are most likely to use when gathering data, and they are:

- Controlled
- Semi-controlled
- Free-form

Controlled interviews

Here the questionnaire is used as the basis of the interview. It is adhered to rigidly. Because the questions are closed, there is no opportunity for respondents to amplify or clarify their answers.

Advantages
- Fast
- Low cost
- The interviewer needs very little skill
- Easy to process the responses

Disadvantages
- Inflexible
- Limited information
- Potential for bias

Semi-controlled interviews

Though more flexible than the controlled interview, semi-controlled interviews still have a formal structure. However, they do allow for some amplification of response on the part of the interviewee and interviewers can probe for answers.

Advantages
- A great deal of good quality information can be gathered
- Interviewee has a greater participation and, therefore, interest
- The information gathered is more detailed

Disadvantages
- Much more skill is required on the part of the interviewer
- More time is needed to complete the interview
- More costs are involved
- Responses are much more difficult to record

Free-form interviews

All interviews will descend into chaos if the interviewer is not trained or experienced. This category of interview is especially susceptible. The free-form interview falls into two sub-categories:

- Depth interviews
- Group interviews

DEPTH INTERVIEWS

Depth interviews are designed to discover motivations behind actions and why attitudes are held. There is a special need for trained interviewers here. The case might be argued for professional psychologists to be used. This kind of interview will therefore be expensive and time-consuming.

GROUP INTERVIEWS

Using groups of between eight and 12, these interviews produce qualitative data. They can be used to get an overview of a training need or to obtain a cultural view of the organisation. These are best carried out with groups that represent particular aspects of the training project. For example:

A group of respondents that have no experience of a particular piece of hardware or software.	Here the analyst can gain an overview of skills weaknesses and the need for training as a group.
A group of Subject-Matter Experts (SMEs).	A more in-depth response can be gained here, bridging best practice of legacy and the roll-out of hardware and software.

Interviewer
It is most likely that the analyst will conduct the interviews. However, this does not mean that the process will be carried out in a haphazard fashion. There is still a requirement for the interviews to be logical and, most of all, structured.

Where more than one interviewer or analyst is used, the lead analyst should ensure that all interviewers are aware of the major points to be gained from the interview. Pilot the interview as well as the questionnaire n order to benchmark the process. Certainly, as a minimum objective the interviewers should be briefed. The data gathering could be compromised if one interview is conducted differently to the next.

Summary

For any TNA there will be two levels of knowledge gathering:

Strategic – this helps you to run the TNA
- Explicit – organisation documentation, etc.
- Tacit – from those directly controlling or affected by the TNA, etc.

Training Needs – specific – this moves you towards the training solution
- Explicit – previous training documentation, detailed processes, etc.
- Tacit – the skills and knowledge of the workforce

Data can be gathered through:

- Questionnaire – yes/no, short answer, in-depth
- Interview – controlled, semi-controlled, free-form
- Observation
- End product

Putting the facts together

Solutions, reports and Customer Relationship Management

The main report to deliver is the TNA report itself. Today we are going to look at:

- An overview of the training solutions that you might recommend
- The content – as a strategic list
- Report writing – general tips on research, structure, grammar, etc.
- Customer Relationship Management (CRM) not the software, but the contact!

It is sometimes the case that a separate Design Specification document is required in addition to the TNA report.

Collecting the data

When you research a report, you are gathering data. You will then analyse that data and turn it into information. More correctly you are turning it into 'knowledge'. You are taking explicit or tacit knowledge from other sources, creating tacit knowledge within yourself and turning it into explicit knowledge. To do this you will need to:

- Research the data
- Analyse the data
- Turn it into 'knowledge'

- Make recommendations
- Plan the structure of the report
- Write the report

Research the data
When researching the data you will need to:

- Decide what information you need. Use the objective as your reference and list the areas you need to cover
- Create a list of specific topics for each of your general areas
- Once the data collection phase has been completed, arrange the data into the order required
- Decide what information should be put into graphic form – never work from graphic to text but use the graphic to explain your text

The solutions

Recommending training tolutions

The training solution you will recommend is based upon the data you have gathered in your research. It will be focused and appropriate. It may be 'blended,' that is a mixture of learning situations, for example, IT and classroom. It may be purely classroom or instructor-led. It may take place on-site at the client's workplace or off-site in a hired classroom.

Correct training solution
Recommended training has to meet strict criteria. As we have seen, it must be:

- Focused on the business, training and trainee needs (objectives)
- Cost-effective in terms of salary, resources, etc.
- Accountable with respect to ROI – including how successfully the new skills or knowledge can be transferred back into the workplace

Issues that affect the choice of training solution are:

- Number of people to be trained
- Aspirations and objectives of the solution
- Resources required and available to support the training
- Organisational support
- Time-scales and organisation demands

On-the-job

Work instruction
A more up-to-date version of 'sitting with Nellie', this solution should be:

- Methodical
- Designed

The task is broken into 'bite-sized' chunks that the trainee can practise until proficient. There are three main stages:

- Explaining the task to the trainee
- Demonstrating the task to the trainee
- Getting the trainee to practise under supervision

Learning contracts

Learning contracts are:

- A three-way process
- Bound within a contract between trainee, their line-manager and tutor
- Adaptable
- For individual development
- For training of practical skills

The contract determines:

- The level of learning to be done
- How and when it is to be done
- Any resources needed to support the learning
- Any evidence to be provided by the trainees to support the learning

Coaching

This training is based on the assumption that we learn from everything we do. It relies upon having a willing manager or experienced peer to support the process.

- Coaching is best with a one-to-one relationship
- Trainee development is supported using problem solving or task completion
- Coaching uses job objectives to focus trainee development

Mentoring
This form of training, commonly used when developing managers, is more role-oriented than task-oriented.

Secondment and job rotation
This training was originally used to develop managers, but it is now much more commonplace.

Secondment and job rotation rests on the belief that staff can be developed by contact with different:

- People, organisations and jobs
- Work situations and environments
- Methodologies and processes

If not planned, agreed (within a learning contract is best) and monitored, this method of training it will not achieve the desired learning.

e-Learning
Advances in modern technology have provided access to many forms of computer-based training (CBT, now classed as e-Learning), which can take place in the workplace, and especially in the IT workplace. By this we mean anywhere where IT is a predominant tool in working practice.

Examples of platforms for computer-based training are CD-ROM, intranet, extranet and internet. They can be very structured in their approach to learning. CBT relies upon:

- Time made available, if training is conducted in the workplace
- PCs accessible to the trainee
- The trainee able to access the training
- Available management support
- Available support, such as on-line mentoring

This list is not exhaustive.

Floor walking

Floor walking is an extension of training initiatives such as instructor-led training (ILT). Used for IT training, it allows the trainee to absorb training in the classroom and then reinforce weaker points through 'expert' advice being available back in the workplace.

On-the-job summary

On-the-job training needs to be:

- Planned and structured by skilled and experienced staff
- Agreed between training advisors, managers and trainees
- Resourced by the organisation
- Monitored and controlled by training advisor, management and trainee

Off-the-job

Training course
This is the traditional, off-the-job, training solution, which:

- Can take place away from the point of work, but still on premises or at a training centre
- Trainees can attend from one or many organisations
- Can take from half a day upwards
- Can be intermittent – day release or a number of days over time
- Needs to be clearly structured with set objectives and learning outcomes

Training workshops
These tend to be participative events, which bring together a number of learners who want to develop a particular skill. They are useful for the development and understanding of complex issues, such as:

- Company law
- Assertiveness
- Health and safety
- Negotiation techniques
- Meeting management
- Knowledge

Distance, open and flexible learning
There are many options amongst distance, open and flexible learning. They provide various means of learning by the provision of training documentation, support material and face-to-face and online tutors. This training can be conducted at a distance and is open to all.

However, the onus for development lies with the trainee. There is a high rate of drop-out from courses of this nature. The selection of the trainees and the quality of the materials are two of the most important considerations in choosing this type of training solution.

e-Learning
See on-the-job. The main benefit of e-Learning is that it can be conducted anywhere and at any time.

Self-development
This is one of the most common training methods of development for managers – the trainee has responsibility for the pace, time and place for learning. Most company support tends to be of the 'get on with it' variety!

Self-development can be very cost-effective, although some courses involve weekends and days on university sites, which can boost expense bills. Introduce a learning contract and an appraisal system:

- Training value can be enhanced
- Goals and objectives can be identified
- Resources may be made available to the trainee

Outdoor development
Used correctly and controlled and managed by skilled leaders, this is a strong learning tool. Examples such as abseiling, river-walking, even fire-walking in extreme cases are used for management development or team-building. This form of training can also be used to develop:

- Communication
- Planning and problem solving
- People management
- Resource management

Blended solutions

The modern approach to training is to provide a blended solution. This offers a variety of types of training, each supporting and complementing the other, for example:

- Instructor-led training (ILT)
- CD-ROM
- Floor walking

The report

The TNA report has to 'sell' a solution to the client or project manager. In simple terms, you will need to make sure that you demonstrate an understanding of:

- *Position*: where the organisation was, where they are now, where they want to be (Aim).
- *Problem*: why they cannot stay where they are.
- *Possibilities*: multiple solutions, plus risks and assumptions.
- *Proposal*: recommended solution, plus risks and assumptions.

The report needs to be supported with information covering the data collection methods, data collected, and analytical methods.

The minimum content and the possible order of a TNA report should be:

- A description of the client organisation
- The initial request for TNA
- The initial business case
- Project plan – this can be an appendix
- Data-gathering techniques
- Data collation tools or methodology
- Account of data gathering within client organisation
- Results of data gathering
- Solutions (provide up to three options), with risks and assumptions stated
- Recommended solution (from three), with risks and assumptions stated
- Appendices with example questionnaire and any detailed data that expands on the data results shown earlier

You could add an Executive Summary, using the major headings and summarising the content at the start of the report. This is useful for those busy project managers and clients. Other points to consider for inclusion are:

- Title page with title and author
- Contents page
- Appendices and summaries
- Page numbers
- Conclusion page
- Glossary – important where technical and 'in-house' terminology cannot be avoided and the report is going to multiple addressees
- Acknowledgements and references

Grammar

Always use plain English. Many large organisations have a 'tone-of-voice' and company style. Writing in their style can make a report more acceptable.

Style

General style
- Be aware of the tone of voice, matching the style to the reader
- Use plain English – using a long word when a short one will do can make you look pretentious
- Be politically correct – avoid all 'isms'
- Explain any new ideas clearly by using examples, metaphors and analogies

Jargon, sentence length and words
Avoid:
- Jargon, clichés and phrases

- Old-fashioned words, such as ' thereby' and 'forthwith'
- Neutral words, such as 'modify' and 'influence'
- Ambiguous words, for example, 'quite', 'fairly', 'worried'
- Tautology and redundant words, for instance, the use of two or more words that mean the same, such as 'combine together'.

Make sure that you:
- Use short words
- Keep sentences and paragraphs short – average sentence length is approximately 20 words (never exceed twice that).
- Use concrete and not abstract nouns, for example, 'transportation' is an abstract noun, 'car' is a concrete noun.
- Use active and not passive verbs, for instance, 'I was trained by an expert' uses the passive verb, whereas 'an expert trained me' uses the active verb. To make passive verbs active, ask yourself who carried out the action in question.

Important checks

Always run the spell-checker in your word-processor (make sure that you are set to the language of the reader – English US or UK). Check, and then get someone else to check, your:

- *Spelling*: your choice of words and any abbreviations.
- *Punctuation*: such as capital letters, colons, apostrophes, etc.

Is it readable?

It is always a worthwhile exercise to ask someone else to read through your report to check the flow and logical progression. Data can be displayed in a variety of graphs, charts and flow charts, for example:

Graphic	Function
Bar charts	Comparing items – values (in bars) are horizontal, categories are vertical, emphasises values
Bar or dot charts	Association
Column charts	Frequency distribution – categories are horizontal, values (in columns) are vertical, emphasises variation in time
Column or line charts	Comparing time series
Detailed flow charts	How work moves between operations
Pie charts	Component comparison
Schemaic flow charts	Outline of the stages of a process or project
Work-flow charts	Site movement of people or work

Customer Relationship Management (CRM)

Customer Relationship Management, as defined within this book, is not the electronic CRM database but the day-to-day personal service that you will provide as an analyst and consultant. For example this may include keeping in touch with your client and project manager.

Regular reports
At the project plan stage you need to agree with the client how often and how detailed your reports should be. The client may not want full weekly reports, but you should at least e-mail the client or project manager on a weekly basis (as you would keep any management team informed). A simple way of looking at this process is by asking yourself: 'Who should I tell what, today?'

Looking after your customers
There is more to Customer Relationship Management than simply regular reports, although they do go a long way towards keeping the customer satisfied.

In order to stay on the right side of a client:

- Be professional at all times
- Be honest when making promises
- Be on time for meetings and appointments
- Meet deadlines
- Give a little more than expected

A maxim that can be offered is: 'Promise little, achieve a lot!'

Training Needs Analysis over? Think again!

It seems that once you have completed the TNA and handed your report(s) over to the client or project manager, the TNA is over. Wrong!

We have discussed the need for evaluation in order to ratify the success of the training, and we have looked at the planning, preparation and conducting of the TNA and its evaluation. Now we need to look at the actions that support the training and evaluation, and who is responsible for what.

The client's role

The client has a responsibility to prepare for the training and evaluation by:

- Deciding how the training event will:
  - Benefit staff
  - Improve performance
  - Support business objectives and needs
- Communicating expectations and goals for training
- Finding out staff needs and interests
- Planning follow-up practice and behaviour activities to reinforce new or changed behaviours
- Providing input to the training design, as requested
- Offering ideas for evaluation and follow-up support

Training staff's role

The training staff should:

- Follow good training development practices
- View the trainee's manager as an important internal customer, critical to the success of the follow-through

The analyst's role

The analyst should:

- Gain agreement from the client for evaluation
- Plan for evaluation from the earliest point in the TNA spiral
- Prepare pre-training assessment, if required
- Ask the client to sign off any material
- Remain as SME throughout development and delivery, to detect any fluctuations in content which might affect evaluation
- Conduct evaluation

Post-evaluation

It is not uncommon for the analyst, client or project manager to discover that, after evaluation has taken place, there is a need for more training because a related business need has been exposed by the training. If that is the case, then round you go again!

Summary

The success of training lies not only with the analyst. There is a responsibility on the trainee to prepare and take the training seriously, and there is a responsibility on the client and line manager to support the training with time and resources.

The analyst should plan, conduct and evaluate the whole process in conjunction with the major stakeholders within the client's organisation. However, although the analyst is the subject matter expert, there is no excuse for the client or project manager not being able to understands the TNA process.

The purpose of this book has been to provide trainers with the ability to conduct a TNA, project managers, clients and managers with the ability to understand, set realistic expectations and objectives, and support a TNA. To that end we have just spent:

Sunday – defining the TNA and looking at changes that create business needs and training needs

Monday – looking at the steps that form the process or model TNA and provide process, consistency and quality

Tuesday – planning our TNA and being aware of the milestones and deliverables

Wednesday – looking at where to plan, to prepare and conduct evaluation

Thursday – collecting the facts by interviewing and using questionnaires

Friday – selecting appropriate, focused solutions and writing our report

Saturday – discovering that it is not all over once we hand in our TNA report

SUN

MON

TUE

WED

THU

FRI

SAT

For information

on other

IN A **WEEK** titles

go to

www.inaweek.co.uk